40-Something & FRIED

DARCIA KUNKEL

40-Something and Fried
Copyright © 2017 by Darcia Kunkel

ISBN-10: 0-9985506-1-2
ISBN-13: 978-0-9985506-1-9

No part of this publication may be reproduced, stored in a retrieval system, or transmitted in any form or by any means, electronic, mechanical, photocopying, recording, or otherwise without written permission of the Publisher.

For information regarding permission, write to:
The Zebra Ink
Publisher@thezebraink.com

The Zebra Ink
3896 Dewey Avenue #196
Rochester, NY 14616

www.thezebraink.com

Printed in the United States of America
Copyeditor: Sheila Kennedy
Cover Design: Michelle Radomski
Interior Formatting: OneVoiceCan.com

*This book is dedicated to my family.
Thank you for believing I could
change my stars.
Always have faith; follow your heart;
and pursue your passion!*

Acknowledgments

I want to thank the following people for their help in launching this book: Sheila Kennedy for giving me wings; Michele Patterson and Theresa Pedersen for keeping it real and providing feedback; Douglas Brauner Photography for making me look not so 40-something and fried; and Michelle Radomski for talented layout and graphics choices.

Gratitude to my family and lifelong friends – you know me best, and love and support me anyway!

A special appreciation for all military spouses, both past and present. Words fail to describe the bond I have with you. There are too many to name individually, but you know who you are. You sustain me; encourage me; and have become my closest allies. Keep the home fires burning, and know that you will always be my kindred spirits.

Kudos to my dear forty-something friends – you are my inspiration, mirror and sounding board.

Contents

Introduction: Clichés and All That Crap ---------------------- ix

1: Work = Wine Out of A Mason Jar -------------------------- 1

2: Volunteer Vacuum: Coffee Groups, PTOs & Mommy Clubs -- 7

3: Tweens and Teens: God's Payback ------------------------ 17

4: Relatively Speaking: Family Ties That Bind --------------- 23

5: The "S" Word and Your Significant Other ----------------- 31

6: Frugal and Fabulous ------------------------------------- 35

7: Lost Art of Cooking the Happy Meal ---------------------- 41

8: Glam, Bam, Thank You Ma'am! --------------------------- 49

9: Yoga Pants, Mom Jeans and Muffin Tops ----------------- 55

10: Big Butts, Droopy Boobs and Cankles ------------------- 61

11: Sports Moms and Minivans ----------------------------- 69

12: There Goes the Neighborhood --------------------------- 77

13: Facebook and Frenemies -------------------------------- 83

14: Music Lessons, Pets and Birthday Parties: Oh My! ------- 91

15: Something's Got to Give Besides my Mom Jeans -------- 97

16: One Step Away From Prozac --------------------------- 101

17: Angels with Broken Wings Can Still Fly ---------------- 105

Introduction

*"Every age can be enchanting,
provided you live within it."*
Brigitte Bardot

Clichés and All That Crap

I woke up this morning and realized that I am fortysomething and fried! Admitting to being in my mid-40s is not something that comes naturally to me. Have I become a cliché like so many women of my age that have gone before me? Burned out from child-rearing and lost dreams? Is the highlight of my day meant to be "wine o'clock"? Am I the mom in the bathrobe at the bus stop? Or, maybe I am destined to pass on my dreams to my children in the hope that one of them may dare to fulfill them. Will I get another chance, or succumb to the quiet desperation that

I see in the faces of so many women my age? Can I break out of the façade of the cocoon I have created for myself? It is comfortable at times, but will it help me fly?

These are some of the questions I fixate upon on a daily basis. Where did my MOJO go? I think the last time I saw it was in the mid-nineties. Maybe I can stay at home and sit on the couch with my dogs, catch up on my DVR recordings, and stalk Facebook... yeah right, that happens on a little show I call Fantasyland. When will it be my turn?

Do other 40-somethings out there feel the same, or am I a lone tattered reed in a sea of perfect flowers that have it all together? I wrote this book because I don't think I am alone. I want you to know that it is ok to embrace the struggle, the pain, the insanity AND the joy! I am right here with you. This is not a self-help book, but rather therapy by co-misery.

At this point, one dog looks up at me and seems to wink, but then lays back down with a heavy sigh of annoyance. I interrupted his afternoon nap with my pensive thoughts and the sound of a chick flick playing in the background. I can't

INTRODUCTION

even take time out to actually watch it or join him in slumber.

There are many days when I feel underemployed, unappreciated and overwhelmed. Others where I am a manic superwoman full of energy, opinions and accomplishments that give me a false sense of supreme control. One minute, I am on my hands and knees trying to figure out what I spilled by the refrigerator and how I can get under there to clean it; the next I am choosing a dress out of my closet that isn't from a decade ago and still fits to wear to some last-minute office party my spouse informed me of the day before. One day I have it all together. I go from one task to another with fierce drive. The next I feel like the biggest failure – falling short of all my imaginary mental goals and expectations... utterly decimated.

Everywhere I turn I see women with perfect houses, obedient kids, fulfilling careers, and adoring husbands. Who are these people, and what have they done with all of the "normal" folks? I don't have picture-perfect kids. My home is not magnificently decorated (for years... home was wherever the Army sent us). I do not have precise ornamental frills during the holidays. My lawn is not manicured and impeccably landscaped. That is just not me. Do you have it all together in all aspects of your life? Then, put this book down, because it is not for you!

My mind keeps racing: what am I doing with my life? I divert my attention from this deep intrusive question by running through my domestic daily "to do" list: laundry, vacuuming, bill paying, dinner prep, and carting the kids to and from guitar lessons and sporting practices. It is easier to think about that list than to pensively fixate upon my life's aspirations or past failures.

I admit that I used to have more sass and shine. I was Sandra Bullock audacious. I was actually fun... the life of the party. Did I have diarrhea of the mouth? Yes, but still fun! Now I am just tired and sad. Some days I feel like it is still there underneath all the layers of disappointment and frustration. I often wonder what my children see. Am I strong and fearless in their eyes, or do they see that I have all but given up? Then again, maybe I should not trust the opinions of two teenage girls and an over-active 6th grade boy.

INTRODUCTION

I know I have to make a change for myself, my children, and my marriage. It is not going to be easy because I have become comfortable in my complacency. It is kind of like wearing an old sweatshirt and well-worn jeans. They feel good, but you know they are so 1989. I am a shell of the person I once was, but I have to look at what I have gone through, and how it led me here. I am exactly where I need to be. Striving ahead is all I can do. Leaving the past behind is what I need to do. Do I have a master plan? Nope. Just the gnawing in my heart that says I have to live and feel whole again.

My former therapist would say to "get out of my head" and free my inner spirit from the neck down. Animals never question what they are doing with their life. They just live it. I should get on with that, but in the meantime, where is that Chardonnay I purchased yesterday?

What is it that makes me fortysomething and fried? Everything. There are so many ways in which life burns me out. That list includes everything from work and volunteer drama, kids, beauty, health and exercise regiments to finances, friendships, crazy families, social media and yes – even owning a pet. Let me explain.

1

WORK =
Wine Out of a Mason Jar

"If you want something said, ask a man, if you want something done, ask a woman."
• Margaret Thatcher •

All work and no play makes mom want to drink all day. Maybe you are one of those fortysomethings who has a fabulous career, no children, a hip dog and a cute young husband. You travel, live in a beachside condo, and have tons of friends and money. Your life is wonderful and fabulous all the time. Yippee for you! No offense, but I am certain it is not all that, and yes, I resent you. Maybe you will trip on your Jimmy Choos getting out of your Lexus. Do you resent me for having a family, a muffin top and a minivan? Not likely.

Whether you are a stay-at-home mom, or work part or full-time, there are still so many stressors that fry us out on a daily basis. I am not here to debate who has a more difficult road, as I don't know your personal situation. I do know that I have played all three roles, and each has its own challenges. Too much time is wasted on debates like that. Let's admit it: we have all had fortysomething and fried moments at different points in time.

I went to college and had big dreams, hopes and illusions. Reality is here. I still have aspirations, but more importantly, small goals each and every day – like not screaming at my kids or refraining from telling the neighbor that their landscaping looks tacky.

Finding the balance among spouse, kids and career is tough in today's society. My mom's generation did not feel this constant need to do everything and be all to everyone. We are daily bombarded with media and TV shows that tell us we can do it all – and do it well. From a very young age, I just knew I would be the perfect wife, the best mom ever, and have an awesome career. I set the bar pretty high for myself, which caused large letdowns when all that did not pan out the way I had imagined.

I am not sure where the notion came from that as women we had to not only raise our children, but to also work full-time and compete with men. My guess was in the 60s and 70s with all the "woman power" and bra-burning going on. You still see it today in the feminist movement and recent marches. I thought we were created to do all the stuff men could not do... like giving birth. You know – the yin and yang thing?

My high school class voted me most likely to succeed, and I was their valedictorian. I went on to graduate Magna Cum Laude. I always had lofty expectations. After college, I worked in the finance sector while my spouse went back to get his degree. Our roles flipped as I had my first child just after he graduated and returned to active duty military.

My paid job ended; I had a newborn; and we moved – all within 3 months' time. I was a basket case with no identity for a while, but then got myself into a cycle of endless volunteer work. Why is "work" always associated only with paid positions? Cooking, cleaning, parenting, volunteering, managing day-to-day household operations and finances = WORK! Why do I always feel the need to get validation from a paycheck? Maybe it's because all those other obligations are often thankless. My family does not even know what I do all day long, nor do they understand all of the behind-the-scenes tasks that keep this unit running.

Over the years, I observed many military spouses start home businesses. They are still the rage, and do generate some extra income. I lost count of how many home-based parties I was invited to including, but not limited to: Discovery Toys, Silpada Jewelry, Pampered Chef, Mary Kay, Wine Shop at Home, Scentsy Candles, Stella and Dot, Thirty-One Purses, Longaberger Baskets, Tastefully Simple, Tupperware, and Origami Owl. One year, I counted seven invitations for the same week right before the holidays. I would often go to socialize, but then felt obligated to buy something that I probably did not want or need. Sometimes I would decline, but then bought something from the online catalog anyway. That is how those parties work. They just were not for me to utilize as a business.

I did have a small catering venture for military functions while we lived on post. It was more of a hobby since I had three younger children, and a husband who deployed for 15 months. Military spouses often struggle to maintain gainful employment. Single mothers also shoulder the same burden of managing everything themselves.

I got tired of running myself (and my family) ragged. There was nothing left to give my kids at the end of the day. Who was I doing it for? My dad —who was disappointed that none of his children followed in his footsteps to become a doctor? My mom and her constant anxiety and questioning "suggestions"? Society, which says I can have it all: success, career, perfect kids, caring spouse? Remember that TV commercial that kept telling us that we could bring home the bacon, fry it up in a pan and never let our partner forget they were a man? What a load of bull. All that did was emasculate men and give false expectations and pressure to young women everywhere.

Prior to our family's move back to Colorado, I had gone back to work full-time as an office manager for a startup tech company. I had a whole new stressor list to fry me out: commute, deadlines, co-workers, bosses, subordinates, etc. The work was interesting, but I must say that managing the house, kid's schedules, finances and all I had done before became a lot more complicated and exhausting. It is not that my family did not step up to help out – they did, but it was just a lot for everyone.

If you are fortysomething and choose (or have to) work full-time, I do not fault you for that. If burning the candle at both ends works for you and your family, more power to you. Who knows, I may be right back in the mix with you at some point. Right now, it just does not make sense for our family.

40-Something Lessons Learned: Work

- Make sure the pay and/or experience are worth the costs.
- Unpaid work is work too.
- Raising kids is a hard job, and the rewards are not often immediate.
- If you are working outside the home, actually use your vacation time for you and your family.

2

Volunteer Vacuum: Coffee Groups, PTOs and Mommy Clubs

"I will get the work done with or without pay."
Lailah Gifty Akita

Who really wants to go to all of those 8am or after school volunteer meetings for the Parent Teacher Organization (PTO)? I don't, but I did it out of the compulsory need to support my kids, and to find out all the latest and greatest news. Bobby's mom goes in her leggings, trendy workout top and sun visor. Barf. I used to think I had to sit on every board and go to every meeting. What was my motivation? Sometimes the squeaky wheel does get the grease, but often I just exhausted myself for a scrap of validation. Maybe you are motivated by truly altruistic visions and love helping others. It's just not for me.

Even volunteering at my kids' schools presents a challenge. I found that as soon as it was known I was not working full-time, a myriad of "volunteer" options (and obligations) suddenly appeared. As groups found out I was available or had volunteered with one organization, the calls and suggestions began. This was especially true as a military spouse. Some people live for it – I did for years.

Navigating the social and political hierarchy of school or other groups like the PTO or Booster Club is a nightmare. I can usually find the important intel on a website. Many of the meeting attendees are looking for something to control (other than their kids), or they seek accolades from others in the mommy friendship club. Nothing wrong with that – it is just not me. I am a bit too blunt and in-your-face for most of the groups. I can't recall my mom ever attending a PTO/PTA meeting when I was growing up. I don't even know if my school had one. There were no room parents. My kids hate when I hover and volunteer for every school-related event on the planet. Helicopter moms should be grounded. I'm just saying.

Fundraising for schools, sports and church can also be quite exhausting. I have three children. All are involved in various activities. Each of these seems to have one or multiple fundraisers. My kids would get all amped up at moneymaking rallies with the promise of cheesy prizes for meeting sales goals. They came home with many items to sell over the years… wrapping paper, cookie dough, poinsettias, wreaths, popcorn, girls scout cookies, grocery cards, entertainment books, etc. With our many military moves, various school districts and sport teams, I can't even begin to list them all.

There are always the year-round obligations of box tops and soup labels to worry about as well. Throw in the occasional restaurant dinners, concessions work, car washes, jump roping or hooping for health awareness, and special event obligations, and your year is suddenly full of solicitation duties.

Many times, we would simply buy products for our family or just donate a check. One of our school districts actually did that: we paid a yearly fee in lieu of any fundraisers. At least I was not dreading the white packet of information on the next latest and greatest way to support. With all of the other school-related scheduled activities like welcome back nights, parent-teacher conferences, band and choir programs, classroom holiday parties and programs, and end of the year celebrations, I now have to prioritize and be a bit selective on participation. I am not saying to cut out fundraising for your school, church or sports team, just be realistic or you will find yourself buying 100 chocolate bars yourself to meet the quota.

Household6 is a military term used to describe the "commander" of the house. That was me for 20+ years (and still is). In the military, spouses were encouraged to be part of the Family Readiness Group, Spouses' Club and Coffee group. While my husband was in command and deployed with his unit, I ran his Family Readiness Group. I basically worked for the Army for free. I was happy to do it. Families needed me, and I needed them. I felt obligated, but also resentful. My husband and I worked as a team, but I took a break when his almost 3-year command was up. When you keep pouring yourself out and never get filled back up, you have nothing left to give. Anger, exhaustion and resentment will fill the void. Your body, mind and spirit need time to recover. The old adage "too strong for too long" applies, and then you have nothing to offer. Problem is, when I fully committed myself to all of these various additional duties, I was left emptied and drained by the time we left the military.

I don't know how many "certificates of appreciation" I have received from various organizations for my "work" over the years. The recognition was lovely, but I always felt like I was not contributing. As my spouse's final deployment was ending, I got my MBA in management through an online program. It was a painful process spanning three years, a deployment, and two moves. Even with the MBA, the notion of a full-time demanding job was somewhat daunting because unless I made a high salary, it actually paid more to have me home. A forty to eighty-hour a week job is not the most beneficial for my family with my husband working full time as well. The hidden costs of having both of us work full-time included clothing, child care, greater tax implications, more dining out/fast food, travel and emotional drain. When I am not straining to generate income, I focus on savings instead (i.e. meals are eaten at home versus dining out; bargain hunting and couponing abound; I transport my kids and clean my own house).

Now that my children are older, and I have another driver in the family, I wanted to get back into the work force. But, again, if you have not "worked for pay" for a while, or are a jack of all trades, part-time or low-paying full-time jobs cost more than they are worth. I once had a temp agency tell me, "You are interesting, but we don't know what to do with you." Fabulous! Thanks!

When I was younger, I often found myself feeling guilty if I did not participate in everything from the latest email challenge to benefit a disease, to school fundraisers to starving children in Africa. I have learned to choose those causes I am passionate about, and not throw myself into debt to help everyone on the planet. Do I really need Girl Scout cookies? No, but I am convinced that thin mints will actually make me thin, so I'll take a box!

VOLUNTEER VACUUM: COFFEE GROUPS, PTOS AND MOMMY CLUBS

Even church, extra work events, and community and social group obligations can get overwhelming. I would volunteer for everything, so then I would be continually asked over and over again for more and more commitments. It is a vicious cycle. When that starts to spread to every organization you and your children are involved in, you end up completely frazzled. Yes, I thrive on staying busy, but pretty soon I did not even have time for my own well-being or that of my family. Prioritization is paramount.

My volunteering had phases. With my first child, I was at every meeting and knew about every aspect of their school. After I had the third child, I got really good at communicating via email and only attending initial important meetings for school, sports, church activities, etc. When you have three kids' schedules plus your own to worry about, you just can't commit to being on every committee or offering to be the team mom each year.

I have learned to give myself permission to say no. However well-intended, extra commitments tend to pile on, and soon your calendar has so many obligations marked in a different dry erase marker color or highlight on your computer, it looks like a bag of skittles threw up on it. When I have too much going, I find myself rushing from one event to another while choking down a pile of fast food. Most of the so-called obligations I regret later. I find myself giving emotional leftovers to my children. I never want to give my kids leftovers. Maybe from the kitchen table, but not from my life. Thank you for your dream-crushing non-vote of confidence. I am not advocating treating them like little kings and queens with every whim fulfilled (as noted – helicopter moms should be grounded), but there need to be boundaries in your life to create a balance within the family, workplace and volunteer worlds.

I want to curl up in the fetal position and take a nap, but I have to pick up my daughter from high school, son from elementary school and hit my other high school daughter's softball game. Maybe tomorrow I can sneak one in. Yeah, right!

40-Something Lessons Learned: Volunteering

- It is ok to say no – it gives someone else the chance to step up.
- Volunteering is work too.
- Sometimes taking a lesser role instead of the lead encourages others, and lessens stressors and obligations.
- Recognize burn-out and resentment. Give yourself permission to decrease or walk away from some commitments.
- Be present in your family's lives. Set boundaries to find balance.

3

Tweens and Teens – God's Payback

"Never lend your car to anyone to whom you have given birth."
— Erma Bombeck

My days of breast-feeding and diaper changing are over, but the exhaustion continues with tweens and teens. Maybe that is not you, and you are still in the thick of it. You may have gotten a surprise baby later in life, or planned everything so that you had babies after you had a career. Your time will come… you'll probably be 50-something and even more fried.

I was by no means really young when I had my first baby at age 27 and my last at age 33. At least I am no longer obsessed with whether I should bare the boob in public; the choice to use disposable versus "natural" diapers; or if I should make my own baby food. Some people get really stressed out over those types of decisions. I sort-of used to be one of them.

I have migrated beyond baby and toddler tantrums to tween and teen drama. It is one of the hardest ages to handle on the mommy spectrum and often a thankless job. It is kind of a crap shoot. You never know what you will get from day to day. One might be having a hair emergency, while the other is failing math.

Everything from keeping their rooms and bathrooms clean, to dating to getting their driver's license freaks me out. Even my 12-year old son has girls texting him already! I am fortunate that said child still wants to give me an occasional hug. My heart is a little sad knowing that soon he will blow me off like his older sisters. Maybe he will be a momma's boy, but truthfully – I do not want a jobless 30-year old living in my basement!

Not only do I have to be stressed about today's social media for myself, but also for my kids. I often feel like Big Brother, and it is not something I had to deal with as a kid. I barely had MTV let alone a phone and a computer in my hand all of the time. Generations are now distracted from life and relationships by the latest and greatest new shiny technological advance – from watches to phones to television to virtual reality. Feels like I am in the twilight zone.

Most days, I have three mini-me clones on a payback mission. Do you have a first-born bossy child? I do. She is the reliable one that takes control of any situation. My middle child is constantly suffocated by the two strong personalities of her older and younger siblings. She is the drama queen. The youngest one is the smarty pants that gets away with much more than his two older sisters… at least that is what they insist. He is the showman.

My husband and I are soldiering on within the uncharted territory of parenting teens and tweens. So many things to freak us out: driving permits, licenses and car purchases; bullying issues; weight issues; educational progress; religious training; sports schedules and drama; last minute science projects; birthday parties; college choices; and prom and other hormone-filled dances. I could write another book on fried-out parenting… no wonder I am frazzled.

There also seems to be the endless stream of money that is tied to each of these bundles of joy. Costs include everything from clothing, makeup and hygiene products to car insurance, college savings and spending money. I will give them kudos for contributing to their purchases through babysitting, chores, etc. My oldest even bought most of her first vehicle herself by babysitting all summer long, which happened to pay quite well, and was less than daycare for the family.

I know I have raised wonderful children, but I often find myself worrying about their future in this crazy, uncertain, unforgiving and often violent world. Have I taught them to be self-sufficient individuals with strong moral convictions who are willing to step up and make a contribution in this life? Did I do my best? I would like to think so. To quote my middle child: "I want steel friends, not pillow friends. People who will challenge me, will stay by my side and have strong convictions… not those who are soft and fake with nothing much to offer." Maybe I am getting it right after all.

40-Something Lessons Learned: Teens and Tweens

- Give them household jobs to do for responsibility.
- Encourage them to get outside jobs – babysitting, lawn mowing, leaf raking, etc.
- Set up savings and youth checking accounts, and encourage them to start using a debit card, so they can track their own deposits and expenses.
- Remember that you were once an emotional, scared, crazy, and immature teen too!
- Forgive and forget... often.

4

Relatively Speaking: Family Ties That Bind

"Insanity runs in my family. It practically gallops."
Cary Grant

You may come from a glorious "Leave it to Beaver" family where everything is picture perfect... all unicorns and butterflies. I did not. I am sure I am not alone when I say that I would rather have a root canal than spend a week driving around to visit all of my relatives. Let's face it – families are messy! Mine is no exception.

My married three times on both sides parents are now in their late-70s/early-80s. Our phone conversations consist of frequent doctor appointments, food concerns, parenting advice, intel on my other siblings, their friends who passed away, politics and health insurance. It is mind-numbing at times.

I do not live near my parents or family members, but much of our vacation and holiday free time over the last 20 years was spent carting the kids and a big Golden Retriever 1,000+ miles to spend a week sleeping in my mom's basement; driving from relative to relative; stuffing our faces; and arriving home completely drained and exhausted. Do I really need to hear the condescension, droning, quarreling and occasional shear ignorance?

Due to lack of regular communication with some relatives, I either get a year-long summary of every achievement made by the kids in the family, or flimsy, "How's the weather where you live?" fluff from a drunk uninterested distant relative or in-law who hasn't the foggiest idea of what else is going on in the world. God help me if it is an election year, or I feel like talking about religion.

My motto when encountering kinsfolk is usually KISS – Keep it Simple Stupid. It is not typically my nature to talk senseless gibberish, but I do it during some family visits to keep from driving myself off a cliff. Do I genuinely care about my family? Of course, but some have crossed the line; pushed too many buttons; or are in constant complete self-destruction mode. To them, I dust off my shoes and say Vaya Con Dios!

Would I rather be skiing at Vail this holiday season? Sure, but the family visit has to happen every once in a while. It keeps me partially grounded and helps me remember where I came from – and sometimes why I left! Everyone has a Cousin Eddie from *A Christmas Vacation*, or the crazy aunt who brings a cheesecake to the dinner only to hide it so she can take it home later and eat it herself. My deceased depression-era grandmother used to wrap recycled gifts in garbage bags, and even took the dried flower arrangements off the guest tables at my wedding home with her.

It never fails: someone is always mad at someone else for some recent transgression or an unnamed slight from years ago. You try to stay in touch, send photos and exchange pleasantries. Facebook, Skype, Snapchat, family websites, Instagram and texting have almost rendered traditional phone calls useless (except in the case of my mom and step-dad who refuse to use smartphones, and do not own a computer).

Some families are close even though they are miles apart, while others live in the same town and do not speak to each other. Family dynamics are often difficult, especially if there are bad feelings; past hurts that were left to fester; big age differences; and life choice conflicts. Generational and life experiences differ. There are 20 years between my husband and his oldest brother. The peer group gap definitely exists. We were in the military and no one else can relate... contrasting experiences.

When you get married, you also end up marrying your spouse's family. My husband and I were brought up in opposite households. Educational, religious and political dissimilarities still exist. Even within the same family, there are varying beliefs. In spite of differences, immediate, extended or multi-generational families can get along smashingly. Others will fight like cats and dogs. Today, there are also more blended families. Divorce and remarriage add a whole other level of dysfunctionality. Both of my parents have been married three times. Just trying to see everyone over the holidays is a logistical nightmare.

Being fortysomething, I am sandwiched between caring for (and worrying about) older parents from a distance, and my own children still at home. I, like my mother before me, took on the role as the family "communicator." I reach out and get everyone together. I am the designated executor on wills, and I make sure my dad gets a yearly Christmas calendar with photos of kids and grandkids on dates so he can remember birthdays. I am also the one who always calls, always visits, and always asks the tough questions. Being me is exhausting. I actually had someone once tell me that listening to all the stuff I do every day makes them tired.

I tend to think of pressing and future issues before most people, and in turn worry about them more too. Half of my and my husband's family could care less. They still don't even know what he did in the military for 20+ years. I get tired of explaining and defending our life. It's enough to drive you to drink. Where is that Cabernet I bought yesterday?

As I write this book, the holidays have come and gone. Compelled once again to make the 2-day (each way) trip to visit, we transported all five of us and a dog. It is always way too expensive to fly...unless this book becomes wildly successful. What motivates us to go? We do it because my parents are getting older and don't travel much. It is not our priority to see every other relative in the area. If we do so, we end up driving more miles while "making the rounds" in the region than we do travelling to and from Colorado. We like to see family, but it is mostly superficial talk you could see on Facebook. Everyone seems to have their own family traditions, and some have grandkids that get justified priority over visiting with second cousins.

For years, both of my brothers and I had not even been in the same room. We were never on coinciding visiting schedules. I would see one, but not the other. After almost 15 years, it took my last living grandparent's funeral to get us together for a couple days. It is a shame that death is what tends to get some relatives to reconnect, but that is what usually draws family out of the woodwork. Sadly, it sometimes drives them further apart due to infighting over some old vase or chair that no one wanted to begin with, but is now a valued part of an "estate."

Maybe you and your family live near each other, and all of you are inseparable. Sometimes I envy that – everyone going on a vacation together, etc. I am also sure that having family right next door comes with its own set of challenges like everyone knowing your business all the time. For me, I will continue to be the reliable one and the great negotiator – trying to hold on to what my family has become. As for my husband and children, we constantly strive to create our own sense of strong family connection, so that it may pass down to the next generation.

40-Something Lessons Learned: Families

- See and call them as much as you can tolerate – you never know how much time you have with them.
- Make sure you are not the only one travelling to visit – the road goes both ways.
- Distance yourself from toxic, negative relatives, but love them anyway.
- Make efforts to resolve past issues and conflicts, but do not be an enabler to current destructive patterns.

5

The "S" Word and Your Significant Other

*"Women need a reason to have sex.
Men just need a place."*
Billy Crystal

Thanks to televisions, movies and advertising, women over forty are often referred to as MILFs or Cougars. Guess the media wants to turn me into a sex cliché as well. One of the biggest issues I find with sex is that I am just plain tired most of the time! After working, volunteering, cooking and kids' activities, amorous feelings are usually the last thing on my mind. Both my husband and I decompress with a couple DVRd shows and then head to bed. No more midnight rendezvous after an evening of romance out on the town. Those days (and nights) are long gone. There is the sporadic date night or special occasion, but more often than not, it is lights out by 10pm!

The morning or "afternoon" delight on a day off works out much better, as we are not exhausted and can then get our beauty sleep later. Sometimes coordinating all the kids to be out of the house for activities or at friends' houses does the trick as well. I mean, come on – you really only need about 15–20 minutes total. Five minutes in the shower works too – trust me. Find the time!

I am also not saying to give it all up and let yourself go just because you are fortysomething and have been married for 20 years. Like any lasting relationship, it takes work and communication. Movies like *Fifty Shades of Grey* often distort our view of sex. You can certainly spice things up every now and then without having to break out some weird bondage equipment.

Do you have to buy all of your lingerie from Victoria's Secret and shave yourself from head to toe every day to keep your man? Girl, most men will be on you like a fly on honey even if you are only wearing sweatpants and an old t-shirt with no bra. Men are not as complicated as we make them out to be. An occasional sexy nightie, bikini wax, or mustache bleach might be appreciated, but not required. Of course, continually looking and smelling like a mountain man might not be the best course of action either. Keep it simple, clean and present!

40-Something Lessons Learned: Sex

- Keep the lights on once in a while – chances are he is in the same shape you are.
- Take an overnight date night away from the kids – even if it is just to a nice local hotel.
- Try new positions and locations.
- Wear that lingerie once in a while.

6

Frugal and Fabulous

*"Being frugal does not mean being cheap!
It means being economical and avoiding waste."*
Catherine Pulsifer

Having a background in business, I handle most of the spending, saving and investing in our family. Talk about an area in life that can cause major issues. I find that being frugal can also be fabulous!

In terms of saving money, I am not one of those extreme couponers you see spending nothing for $500 worth of groceries. However, do I use coupons and shop deals when I can? You bet! There is nothing wrong with buying and selling items on your local yard sale website, Facebook, Craigslist or eBay either. It has also been beneficial for my kids to learn the savvy art of resale and how to find a discount. My son was thrilled to make $35 on old Xbox games he no longer used, and my daughters now use coupon apps on their phones to save. Funny how that happens when they get their own youth checking and savings accounts – good tools to get your children learning the value of money.

I don't go nuts with coupons, rebates and sales, but I do my research. Many times, just calling and asking to update your phone or TV plan will reduce your bill. It is cheaper for a company to retain a current customer than to gain a new one, and they will reward loyalty. I also no longer fall for the daily department/clothing store sales notices that arrive in my email inbox every morning. The deals aren't that much different from week to week. If you can stack them during the holidays... even better. When I need a large ticket item, I will take the time to compare retailers, rates and price-matching options. Reviews are great too. Reading expert and customer comments helps me avoid buying a cheaper item that I will need to replace in less than a year.

Holiday and birthday shopping can be the worst! My kids now hold off on some of their more expensive desires so that they can shop the deep after-holiday discounts. It does not make us weird or cheap. It just makes us smart! Teach someone to fish instead of giving them the fish, right? Sorry, but I don't want 26-year-old "children" living in my basement because they do not know how to make, save or spend money!

It is also not always about how much money you make, but rather, about the process. Take the yard/garage sale for instance. Sometimes I have several larger ticket items like furniture, washer/dryer set, mowers, or lots of electronics. That happened on our last move, which was more of a moving sale. In that case, you may make a bunch off a few items. More than likely, a few hundred dollars is a good yard sale. Everyone wants something for nothing... and that is great. In that case, volume is the key. Sell 300 pieces of clothing at $0.50 each and you just made $150 (along with getting rid of clothes you would have donated or thrown away). My kids like to set up separate tables for their own items, or make lemonade/desserts to sell. They arrange and market the items, and then keep most of the profit. I do take a small fee for doing most of the big work.

Dining out is always a challenge on a budget. I like to only eat out once a week or so. My husband usually takes leftovers or sandwiches to work, while I eat what is in the fridge. I enjoy cooking and grilling out too. A family of five gets pricey, and I do use restaurant coupons and rewards programs (phone apps are great for that). That way, my kids are not addicted to eating out, and I am not broke. We can have a steak dinner and a bottle of wine at home versus using the entire weekly grocery budget on one dinner. I am not a total tight wad. Special occasions do require a splurge. But, with rewards, deal of the day, or selective menu choices, we end up spending less while still enjoying the experience. Even 5-star restaurants have deals now and then. My butt is not as big either because I know what I make at home is healthier!

I admit that I also do some shopping at Wal-Mart, Sam's Club and Costco. No, I don't appear on the "people of walmart.com" site, but I can find deals there. Hey, if movie stars can get a rollback price, so can I! What can I say... I love cheap thrills! I use store coupons, sales ads, electronic coupons and Catalina (those coupons the register spits out at you after your purchase) combos. Stacking them can save you a bunch. Often, store brands with added coupons slash your bill. In-house brands, like Kroger's, can be just as good as name brands. Are you that fixated on which brand of flour you purchase anyway?

Investing is also essential. Not talking about wild stock and margin trades here, but we have always taken advantage of 401(k) and 403(b) contributions when working full-time, as well as maintaining Roth and traditional IRAs. My husband and I also started Educational Savings Accounts (ESAs) for each of our children early on to help ease the burden of any continuing education they choose after high school. Charity is important too. I am a firm believer in giving... what goes around comes around. Never know when you will be in need! Choose organizations that mean the most to you. For us that includes those in support of the military, our kids' schools and sports, and our church's missions.

40-Something Lessons Learned: Frugality

- Couponing and store brands are usually worth the time.
- Combine sales items and coupons.
- Digital restaurant and coupon apps rock.
- Fine dining can also happen at home.
- Save and invest – pay yourself first.
- Find charities with a personal connection.

7

Lost Art of Cooking the Happy Meal

"I'm frugal. I'm not a very acquisitive woman. I never waste food. If you prepare your own food, you engage with the world, it tastes alive. It tastes good."
Vivienne Westwood

I stopped at the Dunkin Donuts to get a coffee… and a donut too. Don't judge. It has been one of those days!

Cooking in today's hectic world is a bit of a lost art. Fast food has become the norm for so many, yet we are constantly bombarded with messages like: "Go natural and clean-eat!"

Let me run to buy that $10/lb. pile of chia seeds and then frantically Google some easy, kid-friendly recipe that doesn't taste like a bland pile of mush. Wheatgrass, quinoa, beet juice, high fiber, all natural, no gmos, low carb, Paleo, flax, soy, vegan, gluten free, fat free, nut free, preservative free, BPA-free, Paraben free, not tested on animals, the list goes on. The labels alone are enough to drive me nuts.

Shall I fix you a gourmet, 4-course meal? Yeah, let me get on that... right between five loads of laundry (I have one in now), walking the dog, grocery shopping and Googling Martha Stewart for a recipe.

Did I just eat a carb-filled cookie meant for my kid's after school snack? Yep – you bet I did. It tasted AMAZING with my second cup of morning coffee.

When it comes to meals, I try trip to skip the promo Facebook videos, and remember my motto again: KISS – keep it simple stupid. Go ahead and try that cool recipe that you see on TV, in a magazine or from a Facebook post, but please do not spend the next three weeks obsessing about how you suck as a woman because you can't stay on the Paleo diet, or went through the drive-through yesterday instead of spending hours creating the perfect "clean" meal.

I will concede that I am a bit of an anomaly: I actually LOVE to cook. It has been a hobby of mine since I was young. Cooking relaxes me and I am good at it. My comfort zone has always been in the kitchen. Maybe it is the quarter Italian in me. Cleaning? Forget it, but give me a new recipe and I am in heaven. Multitasking? Yes... I've got some homemade cranberry sauce on the stove as I am typing this section.

I actually cooked in a couple restaurants during my college years. I spent a lovely summer on the north shores of Lake Superior cooking breakfast and lunch at the quaint Naniboujou Lodge in Minnesota. The thought of staying there and making a career out of it crossed my mind, but my senior year of higher learning beckoned me back to reality. Maybe I will write a 40-something and fried cookbook one of these days: it's not delivery, it's Darcia.

I admit that some days I struggle to be creative with food options. When my children were smaller, I went to great lengths to make cute kiddie food and special cutouts for holidays and lunches. Now I just try to get good food on the table that everyone likes at a decent time. I confess that my older girls probably got a lot more of my "creativity" than my son. By the third one, the need to make

Mickey Mouse-shaped peanut butter and jelly sandwiches had passed.

I also enjoy cooking shows and foodie magazines, but I used to be obsessed with the latest nutritional fads like using kale, quinoa, flax seeds, beets, etc. When my children were young, I made homemade baby food and breastfed until I was raw. As they grew, I perceived that I was a bad mom if I failed to incorporate avocado, pumpkin seeds, soy milk and tofu into their daily diet. On vacations, I felt guilty if we stopped for a happy meal versus "eating fresh" at Subway. I am not saying my kids now wash down a bunch of pixie sticks with a 2-liter of soda either. I do try to make good choices, but I no longer lament stopping at an occasional drive-through or giving them candy at Halloween. Who has the time or energy for all that guilt? Fads come and go. My kids are still here and still healthy!

Yes, I buy my kids school lunches. Do not judge me. The thought of painstakingly creating three daily bento boxes of intricate food selections from ideas that friends keep reposting from Pinterest onto Facebook crossed my mind. Then I entered my debit card number on the school lunch page and knocked out a month's worth of lunches for my children in a minute. Would I save money packing a daily lunch for all my kids? Would my kids eat healthier if I controlled and portioned everything they ate? Maybe, but I grew up on school lunches and turned out pretty healthy. These days, kids get numerous options in the lunch line – everything from salad and a taco bar, to fresh fruit and TruMoo. The nutrition is so much better than the formed spam patty on a bun, chipped beef or poop on a shingle I had on my plastic tray. My oldest offspring even gets to travel off campus to eat. Just have to trust that she will make a few good choices. Can't control them forever!

Have you had your organic chai, green tea and kale today? Organic usually = grown in poop by the way. Yesterday, I found myself choking down one of those "natural" pressed fruit drinks made of the grossest combination: beets, apple, lemon, ginger and carrot. Blah!

When doing my weekly (or sometimes twice a week) grocery runs, I shop primarily around the outside of the grocery store. That is where the fruits, vegetables, meats and dairy products are located. Think about it: most of the processed, packaged junk is located within the middle aisles. My exceptions are dog food, a few canned goods, frozen vegetables and cleaning supplies/paper products. I will throw in some dark chocolate on occasion.... I am not totally delusional! I just avoid unnatural items like potatoes in a box or shelved pre-cooked bacon.

I am also not a fan of the recent "food arrives to your home in a box" trend. Portioned food and spices paired with an "easy to follow" recipe. That may be appealing to singles or small families with large incomes, but just does not seem to make sense for my family of five. Maybe my frugal cooking side is coming out, but two small-portioned meals you have to prepare yourself that are supposed to feed a family of three-four for the price of half of my weekly grocery bill, does not sound like a deal to me. I think I will just print off a recipe; buy the ingredients at a fourth of the cost; and still make it myself!

40-Something Lessons Learned: Cooking

- Fresh is best; frozen fresh is next.
- The less ingredients the better.
- Eat a variety of real foods.
- Shop the outside of the grocery store.
- Hit a few in-season farmers' markets.
- Skip the pre-made meals in a box.
- Not all foods need to be organic – especially if they have an outside peel/shell – like a bananas, onions, avocados and sweet corn. Save that for meats if you must.

8

Glam, Bam, Thank You Ma'am!

"There are so many glamorous actresses, but you know what? In the real world, nobody looks like that"
Rebel Wilson

I hear about all of these famous women – models, actresses, doctors and business moguls. They do it all and have it all. Really? What about the rest of us? If we don't make six figures, have perfect skin, fit into a size 2, adopt five kids from 3rd world countries and wear Prada, do we suck?

Commercials and advertisements all tell us we have to use this product or that product. It is called marketing people! A Rolex, an Apple watch and a Casio all tell time: the difference is the marketing.

If I use that $100 bottle of anti-aging cream, I still won't look like Angelina Jolie. A personal trainer, private chef, makeup artists and Botox might help, but I doubt it. I am not suggesting banning all beauty regiments and to only wear a $10 watch from a thrift store, but find balance in your life or you will always be searching for the next I-Phone version right after you got the latest one. It is a vicious cycle.

Let's talk about beauty. Boob jobs, tummy tucks, fake nails, bleached hair and Botox... why are we doing this to ourselves? Do we really need a Kardashian butt, because there is a whole lot to unpack there! The need to be a narcissistic Nellie – obsessed with the outrageous is mind-boggling. Seems like everyone I meet wants to impress me with their money, social status, perfect kids and job title. I am exhausted thinking I have to keep up with that.

You know why the DOVE Real Beauty campaign was such a hit? Because it was REAL! Regular women with normal, un-photoshopped bodies stepped in front of the camera and let it all hang out. I don't roll out of bed with my hair in place, and my makeup perfectly applied. I snore, I belch, and yes... I fart. I try not to swear, but it happens. Deal with it!

While I am at it, why are men called distinguished and become more desirable as they age, while women are referred to as washed up old maids? Listen, most of us did not marry a movie star or GQ model. More than likely, the significant other in your life struggles with some of the same middle-aged issues you do: weight gain, wrinkles, loss of muscle tone, belly bloat and grey hair. That does not sound very "distinguished" to me.

Do all women of a certain age go looking for the fountain of youth? You know what I am talking about: exercise fanatics, yoga gurus, nutritional experts, Botox queens and clean eaters. I am bombarded with daily Facebook posts, blogs and shares cataloging the latest fitness craze or nutritional remedy that I should get on board with. If I have to see another vegan, clean eating or Paleo video, I am going to puke!

And what is up with the tanning bed? I thought those went out in the late 80s/early 90s. Nothing like frying your skin and looking like a leather orange. Cellulite does not look better tan. Lose the self-bronzer lotions and spray tans too. Who wants to see a streaky, uneven mess after applying that junk?

Fifty shades of grey takes on a whole new meaning as I look at the protruding off-color hairs standing up from my "natural" brown locks. Boxed demi-color worked for a while, but now my trusted stylist, former Chippendale dancer (yes, he really was) Robbie D, helps me out with color and highlights to disguise the rogue hairs. He even hooks me up with a lovely champagne drink during my monthly (or bi-monthly) hair revitalization.

Just remember, there is no need for drastic highlights… leave pink, purple and blue hair to the teenagers! And please, when you hit 40, refrain from chopping off all of your hair because you think you can't rock longer locks. Army egg-head haircuts are NOT necessary, and will often make you look even older.

Along with the graying strands on my head, I also find myself having to tweeze new hairs that seem to have sprouted overnight in places I never had them before. Just like a man's nose or ear hairs pop out at inopportune times, I find that areas of my face, chin, back and chest are now producing occasional twangers. I try to rationalize them by reiterating that my family came from Europe, and all of them have lots of "fur." My Czech grandma had whiskers and chest hair – no one wants to see that. I will keep on grooming!

Manicured nails can be nice, but no need to rush to the salon every other week to get crazy designs or appliques. I treated my girls to a mani/pedi with simple nail colors right before they headed to back to high school this year, but that is a special treat. I enjoy it every once in a while for a gift, but can live without the cost and drama. I remember once getting my hair appointment bumped by a General's wife who had a "nail emergency." Really? What exactly constitutes something of that magnitude? Talk about high maintenance! Think I can manage to file and paint my own nails thank you.

I am also not one to spend $100 on eye cream hocked by a celebrity on the home shopping network – or in the store for that matter. Unless you won the genetic lottery, you won't look like Cindy Crawford just because you bought her wonder makeup. It may help her bottom line, but those creases on your face won't magically disappear.

The last time I checked, a pill to live forever did not exist, so you and I will still grow old. Does all of that over-priced crap actually make you look 20 years younger? I doubt it. Try ditching the cigarettes and alcohol; wear some sunscreen and lose a few pounds. I guarantee that will have a more lasting result than spending hundreds of dollars on high-end make-up. Not being ugly, just keeping it real. Pun intended!

You also don't have to look like a street-walker with layers of caked-on makeup to get noticed. A good moisturizer is a plus. Some makeup works with your skin better than others, but please... save your money for something more practical. Even a few old school home remedies like mayo on your hair or Preparation H on puffy eyes can work wonders!

40-Something Lessons Learned: Beauty

- For makeup and hair color: Less is more.
- Makeup and anti-aging remedies do not fix all.
- Sunblock and moisturizer are your friends; quit using tanning beds, spray tans and bronzers.
- Hydrate and get some sleep.
- Longer hair can still be sexy.

9

Yoga Pants, Mom Jeans and Muffin Tops

"Dressing up is a bore. At a certain age, you decorate yourself to attract the opposite sex, and at a certain age, I did that. But I'm past that age."
• Katharine Hepburn •

Enough about beauty regiments, let's talk wardrobe! Seriously, who wears all that over-priced, weird-looking crap you see in magazines like Vogue? Models in Milan? If I showed up to the next PTO meeting wearing a flamboyant feathered teal outfit with a see-through back, studs on the front, jackboots and no bra, I would have the morning coffee group asking if I was off my meds. What ever happened to real clothes for real women?

I used to be cool with my Bon Jovi 80s hair, half-shirt and Guess jean miniskirt. Now I am stuck with yoga pants and mom jeans. You know – the kind that stretch a bit, or are for tummy control and curvy figures. My closet does not hold hundreds of shoes or the latest plethora of high-end fashions. I have not spent over $40 for a top or a pair of jeans in years. Guess I am too busy dressing my children to worry about myself. Then again, my clothes are not shabby or lame – just classic and economical. I look for good quality items, but get them on sale. I should have been on an episode of *What Not to Wear.* Well, maybe I am not that bad, but my wardrobe could use that $5,000 makeover, while I get a free trip to New York.

While I can no longer fit into my hip sorority clothing from college (shout out to my KKG sisters), I still want to look somewhat trendy. I do not own hundreds of fancy scarves and accessories, nor do I don clogs or stilettos. However, a few good-fitting pairs of jeans and several cozy sweaters can go a long way. I no longer troll Aeropostale, Hollister, American Eagle, Express or Forever 21, but I am not ready for stretchy waistband polyester pants or velour sweat suits with cats and seasonal prints on them either. I do find that the Loft, Ann Taylor, Talbots, JC Penny, Kohl's, Macy's, etc. seem to cater to ladies my age. I try to shop in a variety of stores and online, not only for choices, but also to find great deals. Clothes don't have to have a high-end nametag. They just need to fit and be practical.

I don't know about you, but I just can't pay $200 for a shirt or $500 for a pair of boots. I admit it: my kids are better dressed than me. Most of the clothes in my closet are at least 4-years old. That being said, a few classic well-made items go a long way. Who needs a $1,000 purse that you set on the floor, accidently leave in shopping carts and fill with your kid's used tissues?

Speaking of shoes, some women (and men) are really obsessed with them. I try to stick to the basic styles and colors, so that a few shoes can go with any outfit. I have one pair of moderately priced athletic shoes, cute updated silver Birkenstock sandals, a few pair of boots and flats, and a couple dressy shoes. That is it. Brown, black and navy tones are my friends. Not much into flip-flops either – those are for beaches and nasty showers. They also provide absolutely no support for your back.

I may not be on the show, but some days I do want to nominate other individuals for a wardrobe makeover. Notable horrid forty-something trends I have seen as of late: yoga pants worn as actual pants; see-through shirts (and pants); over-used scarves; UGGS or Jack Boots with miniskirts; cheap flip-flops in the middle of winter; low-rise skinny jeans; jeggings; political dictators on T-shirts; and tiny dogs in purses as a fashion statement. And please, skip the concert T-shirts unless you are at the concert or heading to bed. Hair bands from the 80s should stay on YouTube videos and not as part of a 40-something's daily wardrobe!

It seems like everyone is either trying to cover it up with oversized non-fitting garments, or letting it all hang out with skimpy see-through items. Neither option is flattering for fortysomethings – I don't care how great of shape you are in. The undergarments are just as bad. Buy underwear that fit. A good bra does wonders. Body-shapers are not necessary. I once bought SPANX to wear under a formal dress. The thing snapped at the crotch and was very uncomfortable. I felt like a cased sausage the whole night. I think I would have rather put on a corset that cinched up the back. I am not really even sure how much it hid my love handles and belly flab.

40-Something Wardrobe Tips:

- Miniskirts and booty shorts do not work anymore.
- The pencil skirt is your friend.
- Baggier is not necessarily better.
- Colors can be fun, but you can't go wrong with black.
- Used in moderation, scarves are a plus.
- Accessorize, accessorize, accessorize.
- Stilettos and clogs are a no no.
- Invest in a good bra.
- Buy shoes with decent support.

10

Big Butts, Droopy Boobs and Cankles

"The same ten minutes that magazines urge me to use for sit-ups and triceps dips, I used for sobbing."
– Tina Fey –

Once I hit forty, I realized that my body did not want to cooperate anymore. Gravity has really taken hold – of my boobs, my butt and my face. My once soft smooth skin now shows off age spots and wrinkles. Even my vision has changed. I got Lasik a few years back, but recently strain when looking close and then far away. I am not a fan of bifocals, but I may be headed in that direction.

I am also pretty sure the twin peaks have dropped, and that one remains larger than the other after all that breastfeeding. It could also be from the now-required yearly tata smashing. There is nothing like shoving your boob flesh in between two cold metal slabs and then trusting the machine and a technician not to completely flatten them like a pancake. Important? Yes. Comfortable. No!

Additional areas of aggravation: my muffin top, back fat and saggy butt. I am pretty short, so any weight gain or muscle tone loss is noticeable. I am no longer the tiny flyer cheerleader I once was. The mommy pooch even comes complete with stretch marks and a more pronounced "inny" belly button than before! It's no joke when my pelvic floor started to drop... of course popping out three kids will do that to you. The doctors want me to keep up my kegels. Yea, I will get right on that during my next errand run in the van. I can always add it to my daily exercise "to do" list of shame. I have a Pilates ball from a long-ago class that is great for the core and pelvic floor. I can still do some awesome moves... when I bring it up from its basement home.

I was never a very limber girl. My muscles were never stretchy. Power and strength were more my thing. Now, my neck and shoulder muscles carry the weight of constant nagging stress. My knee sometimes seems off kilter. Popping and cracking can now be heard quite often if I bend down. I should really take up yoga.

I also used to be fairly strong for my 5'2" frame, but now I sometimes catch myself very frustrated at not being able to open a pickle jar. I am not elderly for crying out loud, but the muscle tone is not what it used to be. My 5-lb. weight exercise reps might help a bit, and even walking my 85 lb. Golden Retriever is a good workout. More often than not, my shoulders are pulled out of whack due to a bunny or squirrel sighting along the way.

Yearly doctor visits are quite interesting these days. I happen to have a good-looking medical practitioner. What's that about? It is a bit uncomfortable, but my father was a family practice doctor, and I had three natural births - two on military bases. Everyone saw my baby chute, and at that point, I DID NOT CARE! Shyness is not an issue, but I do feel more self-conscious about my body these days. I never look at the scale when they write down my weight. On my last visit, they made me do the pee test and blood draws. Hitting that tiny plastic cup is always a hoot, too. I even accidentally forgot the lid last time, and spilled a bunch in the collection bag. I am sure the lab techs loved me that day. My bad cholesterol was high... go figure. Need to lose weight and cut back on wine intake. Bummer. Guess I will increase my veggie intake and exercise a bit more. At least I can look at the mountains while lugging my dogs on walks. The wine? We'll see.

Speaking of dogs, when I hear the phrase "down dog," it sounds more like my emotional state rather than a yoga position designed to strengthen and stretch my entire body. I knew several friends who got on the "poopy tea" trend to lose weight. Nothing like chronic diarrhea to get you inspired. I weighed 105 pounds in high school and was a flyer on the cheerleading squad. That was almost 30 years and 30 pounds ago. I would not be caught dead hurling myself off the top of a pyramid in a skimpy outfit today. Will I work out and eat healthier to lose a few pounds? Sure, but I am no longer obsessed with my post-three natural birth body. And besides, my husband likes my bigger boobs.

As mentioned, I used to take Pilates, and enjoyed "working the ball," but now I just have the ball in my house and do V-situps on my own. Planking helps too. Do I enjoy it? Not really, but it gets the job done. Just throw on some music and hold it for a song or two. I stay with the simple basics when exercising. There have just been too many hip workout routines and crazes over the years for me to keep up with: 70s yoga, Pilates, Zumba, Bikram yoga, salsa, spin class, Tae Bo, Jane Fonda, Richard Simmons, water aerobics, step class, and my latest favorites: yoga with goats and the bungee workout. I guess I am just not Zen enough from some of these!

Why do we continue to subject ourselves to these regiments, or jump from one to another? Do we all need to run out and buy the ab roller, thigh master, Nordick track or the perfect pushup equipment? I am not advocating lack of exercise. If you are into one or all of these fitness programs, fabulous. I spend enough time indoors staring at a computer and playing with others. I don't need another room of sweaty strangers judging me or trying to pick me up! I choose to exercise in nature the way God intended: I walk the dog, actually get outside with my kids, run, garden, and ride my bike. Join me in the outdoor exercise experience and become inspired!

As far as overall healthy living philosophies go, there seems to be a wide range: at one end of the spectrum you have high-end naturalists: those trying to be "natural," while everything else about them is unnatural – from their hair to their trendy clothing. The high-enders will be walking around with UGG boots, North Face clothing, and sipping VOSS water or kale juice while driving a new Land Rover. They shop at wholesome food stores, like Sprouts, Whole Foods or Trader Joes, and are into the latest greatest products that are "au natural."

The minimalists, by contrast, live in one of those tiny houses you see on TV, or in a log cabin in the woods. These are the true hippies with their let it go grey hair and Birkenstocks. They drive old Jeeps, ratty Volkswagen vans or rust-covered trucks, and make all of their own products: everything from soap to feminine hygiene products… I am not kidding. These individuals are basically off the grid, and like it that way. They renounce makeup, shaving, jewelry and any type of flattering clothing. I call this group the granolas – lots of them here in Colorado. Their babies are always in a sling. They homeschool and remind me why I should too. Do not misunderstand, I am not against homeschooling (I have friends and relatives who do), but it is definitely not for me or the sanity of my children.

Like most women, I fall in the middle. I own a pair of Birks – they are comfortable and have gotten more stylish over the years. I like highlights in my hair when I can afford them. I am not, however, the other extreme – uber-natural people as mentioned above. Both of them drive me a little nutty. I live in the middle – a realist.

40-Something Exercise and Wellness Tips:

- Get outside and exercise in nature: hike, bike, run, walk.
- Stay away from trendy regiments or fad diets – make lifestyle changes.
- Drink water, but it does not have to be high-end.
- Hand weights work wonders.
- Just because something is expensive does not mean it is the best.

11

Sports Moms and Minivans

"Thank you for putting the family of stickers on your car window, your minivan had me under the impression that you were wild and single."
• Author Unknown •

Nothing goes better together like sports mom and minivans. I drive a Toyota Sienna. It is the workhorse vehicle of the family – kind of like I feel most days. I have had four versions of said van over the last 17 years. I am practical, not precocious.

While I may lose me some cool points, my Sienna will still crush that tiny Porsche in a heartbeat. I don't drive it to make some sort of pretentious statement. I drive it because I am smart! It is practical. I have three kids and two dogs – I need an economical dependable vehicle. Besides, that old bald fat dude driving to the soccer game in the Ferrari isn't racking up any cool points either.

I watch other soccer moms out there who have to upgrade to the latest and greatest vehicle they see on TV. I am not admitting to anything, but I definitely do not need a $60K sports car or high-end crossover to drop my kid off at school in my pajamas. The minivan works just fine for me!

My minivan is also not decorated with all kinds of "look at me" appliqués. How narcissistic can we be? I do not need to feel less than I do because you have a 13.1 or 26.2 plastered on your back windshield. News flash: no one cares that you ran a half or full marathon. Do you want me to pull you over and congratulate you on how wonderfully in shape you are? For safety (and privacy) purposes, I also do not advertise my family (and pets) with stick figures on the back windshield. So your kid is an honor student. Want me to put one on saying "Parent of a C+ Math student"? If you choose to adorn your vehicle with stickers and signs, at least make them interesting, funny or thought-provoking. I enjoyed the last one I saw which pictured a mountain scene with the words "I Like It On Top." That put a smile on my face. Even the nerd mobile with *Dr. Who's* Tardis and the *Harry Potter Deathly Hallows* stickers gave me a chuckle. I saw one recently that said "Trees are the answer." Umm... what is the question?

I used to put military stickers on the van when my husband was deployed. Not really for sympathy, but I guess I was just proud that he was risking his life for my freedom. Naked lady dancers or characters peeing on a Ford or Chevy symbol, on the other hand – I can do without. Does this sound like a diverted rant? Well, it is.

The part of sports that actually really fries me out is all of the "taxiing" in aforementioned minivan that I end up with for all of my kids' activities. I call it tag-team driving. My husband and I often feel like strangers passing each other in our vehicles while heading to and from events. When he was deployed to Iraq and Afghanistan, I had to cart the kids from place to place myself. It was literally like the movie Groundhog Day.

My days were somewhat mine from 8am to 3pm – then, I not only drove my kids to after school events, but also other kids of working moms. Remember, I have three children – all of whom were involved in activities. It simply would not have been fair to tell one child that they could not participate in a sport or club when the other two did. I tried to keep their schedules as normal as possible, especially while their dad was at war.

There is a major reason my kids do not participate in "club" and "travel" sports (besides the ridiculous cost). How do you justify it for one and not the others? How do you balance your life if you do it for all of your children at once? Most kids are either natural athletes or they are not. Practice, discipline and determination can create an athlete, but if they don't have some ability to begin with, it is not going to happen. Just because you throw them in travel ball does not mean they will be the next Michael Jordan (who, by the way, did not even make the high school basketball team his sophomore year). Olympic athletes may train that way, but what a strain on the family unit!

I do not recall these types of all-year-round club/travel sports existing when I was in junior high or high school. When did it become almost mandatory for your kid to be on a club team at age 10 to even make the high school team? Imagine the unnecessary stress and pressure on both kids and parents. These teams often travel to other states and expect parents to foot the travel and hotel bills. Talk about making the world revolve around one child at the expense at the rest of the family. No wonder we have a bunch of narcissistic, co-dependent young adults who do not know how to lose. As a family, we decided to just say NO!

Then there are those crazy sports parents out there. Hey, we all want our children to do their best to succeed, but we don't have to be mental about it. Who needs that drama?

I see so many parent screamers at sporting events these days – even in elementary and middle school. You know the type: loud, inappropriate and obnoxious. They come dressed in the school colors, with face paint... sometimes even in a full mascot suit. Their kids might not even play very much, but somehow they think their antics will make it better or garner more playing time. Just because you bought and "donated" your puppy as the mascot for the local high school does not mean your kid becomes a star!

Nothing tweaks my melon like the mom who screams at the coaching staff over her child not having enough playing time right after losing a game! I actually saw someone do this in the middle of the field, in front of her kid and visiting and home team parents. What message is that sending? You are psycho; you can't handle conflict; and you have no manners. Keep that crap private. Sometimes my kids get nervous when I am even in view during a game. They would also rather ride the game bus home and spend time with the team; not be sports "agented" by their mom.

Then there are the armchair coach parents. They know more than everyone, and feel like their child is a star player. They come to every game; yell all the time; and have personal conversations with the coaches before, during, and after the games. They wear jerseys with their kid's names. They video tape, and keep score sheets for their child's "stats." Yikes. I doubt my kid is the next LeBron James, Serena William, Payton Manning or Mia Hamm. Yours probably isn't either. Not trying to be a dream-crusher, but enough is enough. I cheer for everyone on the team – from the benchwarmers to the prima donnas!

Gossip and chit chat also runs ramped during these events. Some parents never even watch their child or the team play. I see you... sports gossip mom. Judging me because I am not holding a Louis Vuitton bag, wearing Gucci sunglasses, and a school-logo designed sun visor with matching ¾ zip-up dry-FIT jacket. Hey, guess what? I also drive a minivan and paint my own nails! Get over yourself.

Similar lunatics can also be found in dance, gymnastics, hockey, pageants, and theater... just avoid these individuals like the plague! Same goes for the school plays, band concerts and musicals. It is fabulous that your child has a solo or the lead role, but you do not have to make a complete spectacle of yourself by showering them with dozens of roses after the program or hooting and hollering when your kid gets out there. There is a fine line between encouragement and straight up obnoxious over-gesturing.

And just as a side note: who the heck created those game snack sign-ups for events? "Your turn to bring everyone snacks for the game, but make sure they are healthy, vegan, and gluten free!" Let me grab the old standby – a bag of cuties that everyone has to peel and leave all over the field.

40-Something Lessons Learned: Sports Moms and Minivans

- Offer to help, but avoid fanatic sports parents.
- Talk to the coach privately if issues continue.
- Discuss inappropriate sports behavior with your children. Ask them how they feel about your participation level.
- Dress in support of the team, but don't make yourself a spectacle. No one wants to see you in full mascot gear with face paint at a middle school game.
- Take time for all of your kids' activities; do not favor one child's interests over another.
- Minivans are practical, economical and fit 8–9 people. Get over your phobia!

12

There Goes the Neighborhood!

"Thank you, yard sales, for being the perfect way to say to your neighbors: 'We think we're important enough to charge money for our garbage.'"
— Jimmy Fallon

Depending on where you live, neighbors can also cause unnecessary drama and unrest in your life. Living on military bases in the past, I quickly learned the game on the "street." I got asked what unit my spouse was in and what job he held. These were typically done to garner information about rank and social status. Other common inquiries revolved around me – "What did I do?" and "Where did my kids go to school?" Each day, I would see spouses gathered outside sharing the latest gossip. Like clockwork, they flocked together in the morning after the kids went to school while sipping coffee, and then again near the time and location the kids were to get off the bus. I learned to avoid much of that.

These were the streets where everyone knew everybody's business, and copycatters lived. What I mean by that is that the neighbors would mimic landscaping and yard arrangements. Every Halloween or Christmas trend went viral. It was like trying to keep up with the Griswold's. Time to one-up the neighbors again!

I had one neighbor who used to listen to everyone over her baby monitor. She also freaked out about the fourplex apartment's lawn care schedule. I have even seen neighbors with "extra" benefits – don't ask, don't tell! One street I lived on had an older woman who seemed to know all of the latest and greatest information going on. Sometimes the gossip can actually be helpful. If I needed to sell something or find out the best contact for a job referral, I went to her. Remember the game telephone? Keep that in mind when confiding in neighbors, because like family: you are stuck with them… unless you, or they, move. That was our saving grace when we were military.

We knew that the average duty station rotation was two to three years. Sometimes we got lucky, and an erratic neighbor would move after only one year!

Also, be mindful of neighborhood and HOA community social networks and websites. I recently joined one of these sites, and found it to be both helpful and annoying at the same time. Benefits included business recommendations, crime notices, lost pet postings, etc. I had ten responses within an hour of posting that I had teenage babysitters available for childcare needs. The downside was all of the unnecessary rants and unhelpful postings. Make sure to have settings adjusted so that you are not receiving an email or notification every other minute!

Don't get me wrong, we have been fortunate to have some wonderful neighbors along the way. These were the kind you hung out with in the driveway or around a fire pit. I am forever grateful for the neighbors and friends who checked in on me during multiple deployments; who threw me baby showers; who watched two of my kids while I gave birth to the third; and who cared for one daughter while I took the other one and an infant to the emergency room. I do have plenty of good memories of freshly baked welcome-to-the-neighborhood cookies, pot lucks and block parties!

When it comes to the inside of my home, let's just say I am not an interior decorator. As mentioned, I am somewhat frugal as well. I simply can't stress about the latest color scheme fads and furniture crazes. My home is functional and welcoming, without being pretentious. Rearranging and redesigning my home every other year is not in my budget or schedule. If I did, I would have to call *Fixer Uppers* or the *Property Brothers*.

Maybe my lack of the decorating itch comes from the many years of moving with the military. As the slogan states: Home was where the Army sent us. Walls remained white and bright with lots of photos and plaques hung for decoration. This was mainly to save ourselves a lot of trouble, as military housing required that walls be painted back to white upon move-out.

We did what we could with the kid's rooms – boarders and stick-ons came in handy. Their rooms tended to get decorated first. We moved most of the same furniture year after year. It was solid, but not high-end because something always got damaged in the relocation. Our bedroom set is very old with lots of nicks as a result. One of these days it will be our turn… maybe after we get them all through college! Until then, we will actually *live* in our home. True friends don't notice or care that everything is not new and in its place, or that there is some dust on the mantle.

40-Something Lessons Learned: Neighbor

- Know your neighbors and help if needed, but you don't have to be BFFs.
- Block parties can be fun, but not every other week.
- Have a few of their phone numbers in case of emergencies.
- If you have an issue, try to deal one on one and not through social media or homeowner's association.
- You do not have to constantly compete with your neighbors. Individuality is good. Simple is tasteful.
- Gnomes, Christmas lights in February and 10-ft. blow-up lawn ornaments are tacky.
- Classic, simple, timeless interior design prevents the continuous need for change.

13

Facebook and Frenemies

"Life is too short for fake butter or fake people."
Karen Salmansohn

Social media has become today's ultimate frenemy zone. Facebook (FB), Twitter, Snapchat, Instagram = voyeurism and narcissism at its finest. Long-lost friends, acquaintances, and strangers suddenly want to friend, follow, or troll you on social media. Teachers, friends of my parents, old boyfriends, college sorority sisters, first grade classmates, stalkers... you post it, and they will come! Suddenly, everyone is your BFF, and they have no problem commenting, criticizing or sharing. Most of these people I have nothing in common with, nor would they be an actual close friend in "real life."

How many times a day do you check your social media on your phone, tablet, or computer? I catch myself doing it all the time. Then I get caught up in reading depressing and irritating posts, along with the occasional cute animal video. I am a recovering perfectionist who always had to have the last word. That is exhausting – especially on social media. I may go a round or two, but sometimes just have to let it go. Otherwise I face the endless, exhausting war of words. Usually, no one changes their position or wins the argument.

More often than not, the issue is not even important. I have decided not to waste my energy, but it took me a long time to learn this lesson. On occasion, I find myself getting drawn in, and have to fight the urge to make needling comments. Social media is a useful tool, but so often, it becomes a time-wasting emotional zapper. You jump on and then realize that you have just wasted an hour of your life looking at memes, political comments and photos of how wonderful your neighbor's kids did in their last volleyball game.

Maybe I am still too old school, but I am not really a tweeter, though I do have an account. Do people need to know I am at the grocery store, walking my dog or going to the bathroom? Probably not. I have avoided Instagram and Snapchat all together, but my kids seem to love them. Think I will stick with Facebook and business connection sites like Linked In for now.

Do you have FB friends that are "all about a cause"? I do. Every post is about how we need to save starving dogs in Malaysia or something of that nature. Pretty soon I have to click that "see fewer of these posts," and then their message never gets through. Sometimes less is more! Still, I find myself guilty of trying to "educate" people via my posts. I am probably hidden from half of my so-called friends right now!

Many days, posts make me feel guilty that I am not on board with the latest social movement or foundation. There are the vegans, the animal activists, veterans issues (which I do support), breast cancer awareness, homelessness, child adoption, world missions, etc. I am constantly bombarded with how I should be doing more for others, and it can be disheartening and distracting.

Several of these are noble endeavors, and I understand the need to spread awareness. It may be very personal to you, but too often people make their entire life revolve around one cause. It is all about them, and the platform seems to get lost. I can't fly half-way around the world to work for doctors without borders, but I can pick one or two issues that affect my community, schools or nation. I just don't have to tell you about it every time I get on FB.

Toxic posts: just say no, lest you get dragged into an online Facebook debate about whether global warming or God are real. I don't need a ton of friends and acquaintances stressing out my day-to-day life.

So why do I use social media? Well, because it may provide the perfect mix of information. I can limit my personal involvement in someone's life, but still get the occasional important newsflash. If you use these platforms for your business, then you are savvy and also understand the power it holds over people.

I've even seen divorces announced on social media because it was a more effective way to let everyone know at the same time. Warning: if you choose to post something snarky on my page about something I feel strongly about, be prepared to feel my wrath! Every once in a while, I go through and filter (unfriend) people out. The purge must be done!

Even with its positives, social media also encourages the frenemy – a person who appears friendly, but really does not like you. As a military spouse, I moved many times over the course of 20+ years. One advantage to moving that much was that I learned to make friends quickly and then move on from those that are toxic. You do not have to accept that obnoxious co-worker on your Facebook. If questioned, simply explain that you limit your social media to family and close friends... or just avoid them until they stop asking.

So much drama these days, due in part to technological advances like smart phones, tablets and social media platforms. Posts, texts, and words uttered are pushed out into the world in an instant through the cyber space vacuum. We live in a "friend/unfriend" exposed life. The anonymity and indirectness lets me say things I would not normally say face to face. I've had "friends" of "friends" reply back to a comment I made on the original FB friend's page. Now I am arguing with a total stranger, which is ridiculous and causes even more anxiety!

It is a tough and often painful lesson for kids to learn as well. Reposting or tweeting something can result in a firestorm that is not easily undone. Something you thought was funny may be taken out of context without body language or social cues. We are creating a society that does not even know how to act or react face to face. I am often guilty of mindlessly trolling Facebook to distract me from my responsibilities or to tolerate the monotony of daily life. The problem is that I often become angry or disgusted after reading posts and comments. There are a few posts that make me smile, but sometimes I end up in crazy debates or rants while trying to "inform" the masses.

I like posts of photos, but do I really need to know what 200+ of my "friends" are doing on a daily basis? I don't even know what I'm doing. Very narcissistic. Does it help people stay in touch? Yes, but it's overkill. I feel so much better when I ignore social media for a while.

40-Something Lessons Learned: Social Media

- Re-evaluate friendships that drain you – no one needs that crap.
- Take a social media break – even if it is just for the day.
- Walk away from argument baiters – hit the "hide these kind of posts" button.
- Get educated about the sites your kids are using, and discuss the pros and cons.
- Use social media for your business, organization or cause to maximize reach, but get advice on how to target your markets.

14

Music Lessons, Pets and Birthday Parties: Oh My!

"When there are dogs and music, people have a good time."
— Emmylou Harris

Other random 40-something and fried stressors: music lessons, pets and birthday parties. They don't go together, but they bug me just the same.

Music lessons can be a drain on the wallet and on one's sanity. My mother's college degree was in music. She was a vocal major with perfect pitch who desperately wanted my siblings and I to follow suit. I think both my flute and piano lessons lasted two years. My brothers did not oblige either. Her hope now rests with my kids. No pressure.

Two of my children have taken piano. Thankfully, we purchased an inexpensive keyboard before investing in a baby grand. That way, when they decided to switch to guitar a couple of years later, we were able to recoup some money by selling it to a neighbor. Two kids currently take guitar, and all three like to sing, so at least that is something. They do not practice all the time, and we drop almost a couple hundred a month on it, but at least they will be well-rounded. Maybe we have an Eric Clapton or Taylor Swift in the making. They can always pay me back if they become famous. That is my justification anyway!

The old adage is that pets resemble their owners. Ever notice that very high maintenance people have little yappy dogs, standoffish cats or exotic animals? I have the trusted, loyal and furry Golden Retriever and a new mixed breed puppy. Not sure what that says about me, but I like to think it is something positive. We are pretty much a dog family, but have had fish and one albino rat we adopted from my son's classroom. The rat did not last long. Rest-assured, we found it a new home with an interesting individual who was completely enamored by it... ew.

MUSIC LESSONS, PETS AND BIRTHDAY PARTIES: OH MY!

Most of the time, I end up doing all of the work when it comes to pets. My dogs stare and whine at me when they need food, water or to go outside. The fur balls do this even if my husband or children are a foot away, and I am all the way across the room. It is like when your kids come to you to ask for help because they have gotten used to you being the one caring for their needs most of the time. When I look into my dogs' eyes, I see sweet souls staring back at me with nothing but love.

I admit that I do talk to my dogs like they are real people, and I swear that they detect angels in our house. Now, I'm not a fanatic about my furries doting on them as if they were real babies. My dogs do not wear studded collars, clothing that matches mine, or bows in their hair. Do I love my dogs? Yes. Are they honorary members of our family? Yes. Do I feed them food out of my mouth or adorn them with more bling than I own? No. That is a whole other level of crazy.

Maybe I added birthday parties to this section because I just threw an overnight soiree for my 12-year-old and nine of his friends. When I was younger, I can only recall a few birthday celebrations other than "family" gatherings. I am not sure when the basic, low-cost event turned into mandatory over-the-top extravaganzas. Newsflash: they are not cheap.

These party ideas always seem to come in some sort of package deal for at least 10 kids at $300 and up. We have hosted a plethora of themed festivities at various venues over the years to include bowling alleys, zoos, trampoline centers, pools, water parks, ice rinks, entertainment/arcade centers, movie theaters, gymnastics facilities, craft stores, and most recently – a Nerf dart wars facility.

I have seen other parents throw elaborate bashes complete with ponies, clowns, magic shows, video gaming trucks, paint ball fields, escape rooms, expensive gift bags, fancy foods, makeovers, semi-celebrities, etc. Some go to great lengths to reserve whole theaters or restaurants. I have even seen destination celebrations – where the guests go skiing or on a trip. Kind of goes back to that "one-upping" other parents... who can give the most to their kid.

On the other end of the cost spectrum (but not the pain scale), we have accommodated overnight merriment where the guests hung out;

ate pizza and cake; and watched a movie. These types of parties can be economical, but be prepared not to get much sleep; to spend the next day cleaning; and to return missing items left in the basement.

My favorite birthdays are when we have a family trip that includes a birthday celebration on the road. My daughter's birthday usually falls during spring break, and she often just wants a nice dinner and cake. The value of a dollar is also a great motivator for teens – a day of shopping may trump an expensive birthday party.

40-Something Lessons Learned: Random

- Music lessons can be wonderfully enriching but be prepared for a loss of interest at some point – invest in small increments.
- Pets require lots of time, money and love. Involve the whole family in the training and care.
- Birthday parties do not have to be intricate, expensive or better than everyone else's. Base them on your child's interests and limit the number of friends invited.

15

Something's Got to Give Besides my Mom Jeans

"If you obey all the rules, you miss all the fun."
Katherine Hepburn

I can't tell you the 50+ tasks I complete each and every day. I wear so many hats that I should own a millinery shop. My German grandfather's family actually did. I am a wife, mom, chef, teacher, accountant, author, entrepreneur, coach, support group leader, and housekeeper. I wear these badges with honor, but I am exhausted just thinking about it. No wonder I have lists, three calendars, and post it notes stuck all over the place.

I take pride in my schedules – updating and marking them off as I go through the week. As I mentioned earlier, I have one of those big wipe-off calendars that lives in my kitchen and details everyone's daily schedule for the month. I use various dry erase marker colors to highlight and call out important family happenings. Truth be told, I have three calendars: one in my purse, one weekly scheduler on my desk and the mammoth one in the kitchen. I won't count my phone because I hate digitally tracking events, and then getting the ding or vibrate reminder. Mine would be going off all day long!

Every first of the month, I find myself writing and copying all events in triplicate. Is this redundant, OCD, and a bit insane? Probably, but those calendars and post-it notes are the only guide to know what is going on around here! God forbid my teens (or my husband) put an appointment in their phone and don't let me in on it. As soon as I find out: on the calendar it goes! They usually get a scolding for not informing me sooner. Same goes for those fliers that come home from school, or the new parent portals that send push notifications regarding every "save it" date. Meeting on this day. Sporting event the same day. Bring snacks on the next day. After careful date-filtering, up on the calendar they go!

Most of the time it is just me reminding the rest of the family on a daily basis. I feel like a schoolteacher when asked what we have today. I say: "Did you look at the calendar?"

I am someone who notices everything all of the time- when the toilet paper is low, if the dogs need to be fed, and what items are low in my refrigerator and pantry right now. Multi-tasking is an understatement. Even when I worked full-time, I still did laundry, grocery shopping, cooking, finances and the majority of the cleaning. Maybe that is because I take control by nature, or maybe I have trained my family to expect me to do it. This happens in the volunteer and work world as well: when you are good at many tasks, everyone keeps asking you to do more, and assumes you will say yes. Pretty soon, you are tired, overwhelmed and angry.

40-Something Lessons Learned: Organization and Boundaries

- Schedules and calendars are helpful… as long as everyone in the family contributes to and acknowledges them.
- Commitment boundaries need to be set to minimize the "skittles throw up" on the calendar. Often, less is more.
- Cut yourself some slack, and encourage family accountability for events and promises.
- Embolden children with chores – even teens can clean their own bedrooms and bathrooms, help with cooking, and do laundry. These skills encourage flight from the nest when they become adults.

16

One Step Away From Prozac

"Well-behaved women seldom make history."
Laurel Thatcher Ulrich

Goodhearted individuals always tell me to stop worrying so much. Easier said than done. I feel like women are natural worriers. Anxiety creeps in and we do not even realize it. Some days the cylinders are all firing and I accomplish fifty tasks. Others, I forget to brush my teeth, neglect to feed the dog and leave the old K-Cup in the Keurig. Am I one step away from crazy?

The older you get, the more information and memories get stored. I can remember the words to every song from the 1980s, but often can't remember a name or place. I have found my car keys in the bathroom, and recently left my purse in a shopping cart on a military base. Too much on my plate.

I think I do have OCD and mommy ADHD. As mentioned, I notice everything, and constantly jump from one thing to another. It is really hard to get into a sexy mood when I just realized that my electric toothbrush head needs to be replaced, and then race to put it on the next shopping list before I forget. The horror of not replacing it on time leading to poor dental care is troubling. Wait! Do I have a coupon for that? No, that was for dog food. Is the dog out of food? There you have it – within a span of two minutes, I have gone from sex to toothbrushes to dog food. Sometimes I feel like Robert Downey, Jr. in the Sherlock Holmes movies – seeing everything all the time, but often in slow motion.

Recently, I was waiting for a follow-up appointment with my regular doctor when I saw the clinic's psychologist. He walked over and said "Are you waiting for me?" I calmly said, "No, but I probably should be."

I sometimes see people walking around who are but a shell of themselves, and I often think: what happened to them? Why are they so sad and miserable?

The stripping of the soul and the dying of the light do not happen in a day, but more often to the slow methodical drumbeat of daily life. I am always doing for others rather than myself. One day I woke up, and those lofty dreams and the vivacious energy of my youth are now but a glimmer – a small flicker of light that keeps me just hopeful enough.

Someday, my time will come. Once the kids have grown. After my parents are gone. When my spouse finally settles in his career. But then I turn once again to my dogs lying next to me snoring on the bed and realize: it is someday. What contribution have I made? Have I used my talents to the best of my abilities, or have I consistently chosen the path of least resistance? God forbid if I ever have to start dating at this age. I am just not sure what that would look like. All of these are the thoughts that muddle through my mind as the winter of my 45th year wanes.

40-Something Lessons Learned: Getting Through the Day

- It is what it is. Life will happen. Joy will happen. Sadness will happen. Keep living and push through.
- Sometimes you may need help with anxiety – especially if it is affecting your relationships and work. There is no shame in asking for help.
- Everyone needs a "daycation" – have nothing on the calendar for one day. Go shopping. Eat out. Sleep. Read. Exercise.
- Coffee and wine are good – in moderation.
- Breathe deeply – it actually does wonders and refocuses your mind.

17

Angels with Broken Wings Can Still Fly

"Always be a first-rate version of yourself, instead of a second-rate version of somebody else."
— Judy Garland

The broken pieces of a mirror may not be pretty or uniform. They may also possess seemingly sharp edges. However, will they not still continue to serve their original purpose: to reflect that which is placed in front of them? Is a mirror being held up to your life? Does it reflect an angel with broken wings?

I am one of those clipped-winged cherubs. I have been told that I have an "intense personality." Translation: annoying, know-it-all, opinionated and overbearing. I can take a hint. Often, I am the only one in the room who actually says what everyone else is thinking, but is too politically correct to say. I will be the first to admit, that while somewhat satisfying; this approach may not produce a desired outcome, and often does not garner you many friends. No one has ever accused me of being quiet, so today (and everyday) I speak out.

If I am being honest, there are many days when I am not a fan of how my life turned out. I get so sick of playing the game and keeping up appearances. It is exhausting.

I used to set my expectations so high for myself, my spouse, my children and others, that I blocked myself and everyone around me. I got burned out trying to be everything to everybody.

But then, I look at my kids, and all of the hope they have in their eyes – I don't want to squash that optimism. I thank God for them, and that the sun still rises – giving me another day to still pursue my dreams. Yes, you heard me – being grateful for what I have been given and helping others is the key. If Prozac or a glass of wine helps from time to time… so be it!

When you are going through hell, keep going right? Need inspiration? Try *The Fight Song* by Rachel Platten...

> *"Like a small boat*
> *On the ocean*
> *Sending big waves*
> *Into motion*
> *Like how a single word*
> *Can make a heart open*
> *I might only have one match*
> *But I can make an explosion*
>
> *This is my fight song*
> *Take back my life song*
> *Prove I'm alright song*
> *My power's turned on*
> *Starting right now I'll be strong*
> *I'll play my fight song*
> *And I don't really care if nobody else believes*
> *'Cause I've still got a lot of fight left in me."*

I, too, often feel like that small boat on the ocean having no significance. I must remember that small boats make waves, and that those waves make a difference. Each day gives me a new opportunity to make those impressions. While the old adage "too strong for too long" definitely applies to me, regret is over-rated.

How do I keep going without completely losing it or never getting out of bed every day? Here are a few truths I have learned along the way to keep me driving on.

This too shall pass. The craziness in our life comes and goes. Being anxious about it usually does not change the outcome. When I am in the thick of it, I take a moment, breathe deeply, and then ask myself: will this matter tomorrow, next week, next month or next year? More often than not, the answer is a resounding no!

Lose the regret and grant forgiveness. I have watched so many people (myself included) hang on to some past slight committed years (or days) ago. The person who has wronged another may or may not know they have done so. Sometimes it is a misunderstanding, but it can ruin friendships, relationships and family unity. Trying to resolve this hurt can go a long way in reducing anxiety, anger and general "fried out" attitude. If you can't or won't get past it, seek help from friends, family, clergy or a professional counselor. When you finally are able to let go, a great weight will be lifted, and you will be able to focus more on what matters in life.

I mentioned frenemies earlier in this book, but it is a few solid wonderful friendships that have sustained me along the way. That being said, I do not lean on them as much as I should – that is mainly due to pride and the false confidence that I can do everything myself. When you need an encouraging word, a shoulder to lean on or an honest reality check: phone a friend. You don't need 100 friends, just a few at every stage of your life who understand and love you.

Faith also plays a major role in keeping me from being completely burned out all of the time. When the world is overwhelming, and I am sitting in the corner of my kitchen sobbing, I throw up a prayer that by the grace of God I can make it through the rest of the day, the week and my life. I do not know you or your belief system, but I will tell you that in the darkest moments, you can find peace by trusting that there is a plan for you. What you are going through today does not have to define who you are tomorrow. It may even help shape who you will become.

Give yourself permission to laugh and have fun once in a while. As a worn-out mom, I feel like I have forgotten how to truly enjoy life. I get so hung up on planning the fun for everyone else, that an event, dinner or vacation goes by without much amusement. Usually, I am just exhausted by the end. Sometimes I have to actually tell myself to let it go, and relish the moment and the place.

I want you to always remember that you are a beautiful soul who is worthy and loved. You do have the right to enjoy yourself even if you feel like you are a broken vessel or a bird with a clipped wing. You still have a voice, a story to tell, and flight in your future.

Are you fortysomething and fried? Me too… now, let's own it!

"To be nobody but yourself in a world which is doing its best day and night to make you everybody else, means to fight the hardest battle which any human being can fight and never stop fighting."
· E.E. Cummings ·

About the Author

As a former military spouse, Darcia Kunkel has a heart for military families and writes on topics including motherhood, Christian inspiration, military spouse transition, practical cooking and the struggles of perfectionism. Readers enjoy her lighthearted approach to life after age 40 that sometimes leaves them frazzled and frayed.

When Darcia isn't feeling 40-something and fried, she can be found parenting her three children, volunteering, editing books and articles, trying recipes and walking her dogs.

Connect with Darcia and join the 40-Something & Fried Community on Facebook and Twitter.

www.ingramcontent.com/pod-product-compliance
Lightning Source LLC
LaVergne TN
LVHW021355080426
835508LV00020B/2288